International Library of Philosophy and Theology
(MODERN THINKERS SERIES: David H. Freeman, *Editor*)

VAN TIL

VAN TIL

by

ROUSAS JOHN RUSHDOONY

1368

1960

THE BAKER BOOK HOUSE

Grand Rapids, Michigan

The Presbyterian and Reformed Publishing Co.

Library of Congress Catalogue Card Number LC 60-6805

Printed in the United States of America

CONTENTS

SELECTED BIBLIOGRAPHY

The following constitutes a list of the writings of Van Til, exclusive of his many articles in various periodicals. In each instance, the original date of publication, rather than of subsequent editions, is noted. (Inquiries concerning any of them may be addressed to the Presbyterian and Reformed Publishing Company, Box 185, Nutley, New Jersey.)

BOOKS

The New Modernism (1946, out of print)
Common Grace (1947)
Christianity and Idealism (1955)
The Defense of the Faith (1955)
Christianity and Modern Theology (1955)
The Theology of Jane Daane (1959)
Christianity and Barthianism (1960)

SYLLABI

The Metaphysics of Apologetics (1931, out of print)
A Christian Theory of Knowledge (1954)
An Introduction to Systematic Theology (1949)
Christian Theistic Ethics (1947)
The Psychology of Religion (1935)
Christian Apologetics (1953)
Christian Theistic Evidences (1947)
Triumph of Grace (Heidelberg Catechism) (1959)

PAMPHLETS

Has Karl Barth Become Orthodox? (1954, out of print)
Letter on Common Grace (1955, out of print)
Particularism and Common Grace (1955)
The Dilemma of Education (1954)
The Intellectual Challenge of the Gospel (1950 in England, 1953 in U. S.)
Paul at Athens (1954)
Why I Believe in God (1948)
Christian Philosophy (1956)
Witness Bearing and Common Grace (1956)

SEE ALSO

C. Van Til, introduction, pp. 3-68, to B. B. Warfield: The Inspiration and Authority of the Bible, ed. by S. G. Craig (1948)
C. Van Til, "Nature and Scripture," pp. 225-293, in The Infallable Word, A Symposium, by the Members of the Faculty of Westminster Theological Seminary (1946)

THE AUTHOR

The Rev. Rousas John Rushdoony is the author of this monograph which deals with Cornelius Van Til. Although written originally for the *Modern Thinkers* series, much of this material was included as part of a longer study, *By What Standard?*, An Analysis of the Philosophy of Cornelius Van Til.

Rushdoony's father, a retired Presbyterian minister, was a graduate of Anatolia College in Armenia and did graduate study at the University of Edinburgh, Scotland. Mr. Rushdoony holds B.A. and M.A. degrees from the University of California and received his theological training at the Pacific School of Religion. For eight years he was the pastor of the Western Shoshone Mission of the Presbyterian Church (USA) at Owyhee, Nevada, and from 1953 to 1958 of the Trinity Presbyterian Church (USA), Santa Cruz, California. At present he is the pastor of the Orthodox Presbyterian Church, Santa Cruz.

In addition to philosophy and theology, Mr. Rushdoony's scholarly interests extend to education and history. His *Intellectual Schizophrenia* is scheduled for early publication. In addition to *By What Standard?* he has made frequent contributions to many theological and philosophical journals, including *Torch and Trumpet* and the *Westminster Theological Journal*. He is the editor of the Philosophical and Historical Studies series in the *International Library of Philosophy and Theology*.

1.

MODERN PHILOSOPHY: THE FLIGHT FROM REALITY

The pronounced tendency of pre-Christian non-biblical thought was its issue in a despair of time and an attempt to reach, philosophically and religiously, into timelessness in order to find meaning. The meaning sought, however, had as its presupposition either a radical despair of the world as illusion, meaningless process and flux, or a devaluation of the world as material and hence transitory and inferior. Whether in the milder forms of Platonism and neo-Platonism, or the extremer forms of Hinduism and Buddhism, this element of escape from time and flux into timelessness is characteristic of these philosophies and world-views.

Man remained in time but found no meaning in time, and, accordingly, sought to establish meaning by some kind of link between time and eternity. The Babylonian *Ziggurats* were architectural evidence of this attempt, being giant step-ladders seeking to typify "a *bond of union,* whose purpose was to assure communication between earth and heaven . . . the Tower of Babel is the cathedral of antiquity."[1] Eric Burrows has seen the Babel account as satirical of Babylonian cosmology.[2] It was that and more. The Tower of Babel stands against the background of the flood and its destruction of a splendid world, with the memory of Paradise and the nearness of eternity entering in, and was an attempt to halt the ravages of time by arresting historical development, diffusion and maturation. By a united world order, flux would be controlled or arrested and eternity thereby made manifest in time. The Babels of history are numerous, and their fate monotonously similar.

Against all this, biblical faith was eloquent. "Destruction" was not equated with *time* but meant literally *the pit,* and the very mutability of time could be a source of praise in view of God's covenantal promises and blessings (Psalm 103). Although it was thoroughly true that "all flesh is grass, and the goodliness thereof as the flower of the field," the assurance of the undergirding of the absolute decree of the Creator and Redeemer made this fact too a ground for triumph (Isa. 40). For biblical faith, salvation is not out of time and out of the world, as with other religions, but is salvation in terms of time and the world. It is not an escape from time but a victory in time and over the world. The doctrines of the resurrection of the body and the regeneration of all things

9

makes impossible the devaluation of matter, while the eternal decree gives meaning to time and process. The eternal decree, because it gives an assured meaning, direction and victory to time and process, becomes the very ground of history, and apart from it history rapidly moves to the chaos and abyss of non-meaning. C. N. Cochrane has given a vivid description, in *Christianity and Classical Culture*, of the failure of classical culture to find meaning in history as against the Christian vindication of history in terms of the eternal decree.

Biblical faith and biblical revelation, by virtue of its confidence in and relevance to time, has a perennial contemporaneity, and is hostile to the attempt at timelessness. In terms of this, much of medieval faith was a radical departure from the faith, and, while in other areas the modern apostasy is more radical, its emphasis on a relevant faith in terms of contemporaneity is a Christian impulse if heretical in form and now destructive of not only the faith but all thought. The principle of modernism is that the past must be interpreted, including revelation, in terms of the present by the autonomous mind of man. Certainly, every age has been conditioned by its situation in interpreting history, science, revelation, and all of life, but the modern principle seeks total conditioning. The more total the severance from the past in all its forms and the greater the conditioning by the moment, the greater the merit, according to the more radical exponents of modernism. Philosophy, for example, is increasingly the handmaiden to physical theory and to science generally, and the shapers of the modern mind have become Darwin, Freud, Einstein and Planck. Of these scientists, it may be said that the tensions and contradictions of their thinking are less important to the modern temper than the necessity to re-order thinking in terms of their thought, and the basically philosophical nature of their theory is overlooked.

Albert William Levi has spoken of "the narcissistic subjectivity of all philosophy since the Renaissance: that whether it begins at the beginning, the middle, or the end, it always takes as its point of departure the epistemic properties of the human self."[3] In Hume's day, for the most part, this subjectivity was a cause for dismay, but it has since become ostensibly a ground for joy, and this erstwhile philosophic vice is now the beginning of all virtue for many. Beginning in Kant, and becoming especially vocal in Kierkegaard, the demand is for the radical autonomy of philosophical thought, a demand for rootlessness, subjectivity and relativism. Whatever "reality" is permitted in some schools of thought is exceedingly limited. Thus for Planck, the limit is this, "Whatever can be measured exists."[4]

10

The architecture of the new Babel is closely linked to the concepts of time and the self. The bond between earth and heaven has its nexus in the self, and time is thereby eternalized and eternity temporalized. The self, therefore, to come into its own, to realize its freedom, must, as for Sartre, destroy the reality, efficacy and inevitability of the past. Because of the centrality of the self, the distinction between appearance and reality must be destroyed, for have not Freud and Husserl shown the equal relevance to the self of both, and the irrelevance of this dualism? Orientation to reality becomes orientation to the reality of the self and its modes of communication and decision.

As a result, the traditional concerns of philosophy have been abandoned by more and more philosophers. Art, ethics, religion, politics, culture, all these things are increasingly abandoned, or become the private area of a specialist whose concern is often more technical than essential, and more oriented to academic problems and debates than the issues of public and private life. In short, philosophy is abdicating from reality and retreating into a technical domain of increasing irrelevance. The logico-analytic school has retreated into linguistic analysis, seeking the one language for all science, a new Esperanto for the New Babel. Some, while assuming a thorough-going metaphysics, have denied all metaphysics, and others have similarly denied ethics, and placed the self beyond good and evil. There has been a rebellion against and a flight from the past to the unobligated moment, and also a flight from casuality in the very name of science. There is also a flight from time in the name of time or the moment, and an evasion of the problems of being by the assertion of the being of the self. All these things are an insane flight from reality, causes for examination less by the philosopher and more by the pathologist. The penalty for all pathological forms is enfeebled life and near impotence to outright sterility, and this nemesis increasingly haunts modern culture. Freedom becomes, even for Whitehead, a perpetual perishing, and for Sartre the prized existence of the self becomes a living death, because everywhere nothingness is prior to being. Having asserted with Darwin that all life has continuity, man must now assent to Jaspers' observation that modern man's life has occupation but no continuity. The scattering of the new Babel has produced a division in the very life of man, one which confounds and scatters not only mankind but man himself. Man, now lost in time, has sought to escape from all meaning, and, in art, philosophy and culture generally, techniques have become the substitute for meaning. Wittgenstein's slogan, "The meaning is the use," has

11

an unintended meaning and a broader application as the description of the modern approach to life. There must be no attempt to understand the meanings of things in terms of themselves but only in terms of our immediate and particular use of them. Thus, Asa M. Stryker, in Edmund Wilson's story of "The Man Who Shot Snapping Turtles" in *Memoirs of Hecate County,* was faced with the problem of good and evil in the form of snapping turtles. Was Manichaeanism true, or was indeed God somehow absolute and triumphant? The dilemma was resolved by a radically new approach to the problem of the snapping turtles: from a moral problem they were converted into a commercial asset. The meaning of the snapping turtles became their use in Deep South Snapper Soup. Unhappily, however, the moral issue remained despite the novel use of the immediate manifestation of it, and Stryker was murdered as its outcome. Similarly, modern culture is perishing because of the outcome of all its clever evasions.

Meanwhile, that diversity born of confusion rather than of health prevails. Philosophers try to be as scientific as possible, and scientists insist on being philosophers, each seeking borrowed honors as the only refuge against nakedness. In a culture where a common faith no longer prevails, this is inevitable. Whether it be art, science, philosophy, religion, music, literature, or almost any other field, this condition remains the same. Each seeks an authority outside his field, knowing the nakedness of his own. Theology and the philosophy of religion have been no exceptions. Having so often begun on rationalistic grounds, they have shared in the debacle of reason and rationalism. Having tried to prove Christianity to the unregenerate on the assumption that unbelief presented a rationalistic problem rather than an ethical rebellion against God, these thinkers were compelled to move with man from rationalism to existentialism in order to have 'common ground' with man, their conception of common ground being derived, not from the fact of creation in His image but from man's changing conceptualization of himself. The collapse of meaning and the flight from reality has thus been all the more tragic in that most ostensibly Christian thinkers have been definitely a part of it. Has there, however, been any effective protest against it, or a counter-movement? The answer to this question is to be found in the new philosophy stemming from Abraham Kuyper, and in its development in the hands of his followers, the modern sons of Abraham.

2.

THE SONS OF ABRAHAM

To ignore orthodox Christianity has become the standard practice of its detractors. Any excuse will suffice: at all costs it must be ignored as impossible." Its followers are too few, or else lacking in intelligence and learning, and if these excuses are shown to be invalid, a shrug of the shoulders is sufficient to dismiss the matter. Any excuse or none will suffice. This should not surprise the Christian, who has it on good authority that "neither will they be persuaded, if one rise from the dead" (Luke 16:31, RV). Men are only persuaded as the Holy Spirit, by bringing them to their knees personally and culturally, creates the situation for belief and Himself gives the faith.

The radical cultural disintegration of today, the flight from reality on all sides, the rise of mental and psychosomatic diseases, these and other factors spell out the judgment of God on a rootless culture and on its would-be autonomous man. Man dreams of creating a paradise on earth while rapidly becoming himself a walking hell. At the moment when comfort and leisure have been made a way of life, man has himself become his own instrument of discomfort and unrest. When Noel Perrin asked his 1959 Dartmouth freshmen students for essays on the world of 1985, he found seven of the twenty-one of these privileged youths convinced that life on earth would be ended by then, with another ten sure that overpopulation would be so extensive as to make world war welcome. Perrin concluded that youth "is a great deal more frightened of its inheritance than it would appear" (*Newsweek*, Feb. 15, 1960, p. 25). The fear and the disintegration are clear-cut. But what of the Christian answer? Has not the church also abdicated from reality? Has not church-going become merely a social ritual in which countless millions regularly participate without thought or meaning and in flight from meaning? And are not orthodox Christians to be numbered among the retreating in their surrender of life and thought to the devil, or in their permanent remnant psychology? All these things are true, but not the whole story.

The Reformation principle, forced into a retreat by the Enlightenment and in long decline and eclipse, was re-asserted by Abraham Kuyper (1837-1920) with great power and vigor. Kuyper's influence in primary and secondary education, in university life, politics and literature in the Netherlands was marked, but his international and enduring importance is in terms of his philosophy.

Before and apart from Kuyper, Protestant thought was infected by the principles of the Enlightment and assumed for apologetic purposes the autonomy of theoretical thought. Two fundamental and dangerous assumptions were made, first, the autonomy of natural man and his ability to act as judge over reality, and, second, the impartiality of natural man, who was assumed to be neutral with regard to the God whose throne he claimed and whose word he despised. This natural man, at war with God, still claimed to be beyond prejudice and capable of assessing with neutrality the 'rival' claims of God and himself. Against this, Kuyper emphatically rebelled, pointing out that apologetics and Christian philosophy were operating on two mutually exclusive ultimates. On the one hand, they conceded the autonomy of man, and, on the other, they believed in and sought to establish the sovereignty of the self-contained and triune God. Kuyper began the work of cleansing Christian thought of this ambivalence and establishing it firmly on the ontological trinity. That inconsistencies remained in Kuyper, and in some of his adherents, can be granted but the assured direction of this school is clear-cut.

While not all the Kuyperian thinkers, both at the Free University and elsewhere, are known to American readers, several have in recent years been translated. Herman Bavinck, Kuyper's successor, is known through *The Philosophy of Revelation, The Doctrine of God,* and *Our Reasonable Faith.*[1] Herman Dooyeweerd's four volume *A New Critique of Theoretical Thought,* and *In The Twilight of Western Thought,* are both major contributions, as are H. Van Riessen's *Nietzsche* and *The Society of the Future,* while J. M. Spier's *An Introduction to Christian Philosophy* and *Christianity and Existentialism* are also available.[2] Other works are being made available through the notable works of translation by David H. Freeman. In this country, the central figure in this school of thought has been Cornelius Van Til, whose *The Metaphysics of Apologetics* (1931) was written prior to Vollenhoven's *The Necessity of a Christian Logic or Methodology.* Vollenhoven and Dooyeweerd are the two central figures in Europe, Van Til in America. Despite extensive peripheral criticism, there has been no attempt to challenge the basic premise of this school, namely, that two mutually exclusive ultimates cannot co-exist.

Meanwhile, the school of philosophical thought established by Abraham Kuyper extends its influence internationally, with an increas-

14

ingly attentive audience in the Far East. The sons of Abraham, that is, the descendants and heirs of Kuyper's thinking, abound and flourish despite marked opposition.

Van Til who was born in the Netherlands on May 3, 1895, migrated to the United States as a boy with his family in 1905, settling in Highland, Indiana. His background thus brought together the influence of the Netherlands and of Kuyper, after training in Calvin College and Seminary, with the notable Princeton Seminary tradition and work under such men as C. Hodge, J. Gresham Machen and G. Vos. At Princeton University, where he was given a graduate fellowship towards his Ph.D. through A. A. Bowman, then chairman of the department of Philosophy, he was trained in the tradition of secular philosophy.

Van Til served as pastor of the Spring Lake Church of Classis Muskegon in Michigan, taught a year at Princeton Seminary and then resigned because of his dissent with that school's reorganization. Subsequently, he taught at Westminster Seminary in Philadelphia, later entering the Orthodox Presbyterian Church.

As a prominent and leading member of the Kuyperian school, he has been especially notable in his attacks on the basic presuppositions of autonomous man in philosophy and in apologetics, in neo-orthodoxy as well as in ostensible orthodoxy, and has thus been a controversial figure. Autonomous man has long reigned as unchallenged emperor in every area of human thought, and the radical and devastating attack made by Van Til has seemed to some a shaking of the foundations. This reigning emperor, autonomous man and his philosophy, walks in actual poverty, though clothed with scarlet in the imagination of his followers. And because men often fight more readily for their illusions than for the truth, Van Til's analyses of their illusions have not been happily received. But this unhappy reaction is in itself a tribute to his success.

15

3.

THE EMPEROR HAS NO CLOTHES!

According to an old tale, certain clever philosophers approached an emperor, offering to weave for him a rare and costly garment which would have the marvelous capacity of making known to him the fools and knaves in his realm. Because of the magical quality of the threads, the garment would be invisible to all but the wise and the pure in heart. Delighted, the emperor commissioned the weaving of the royal robes at great cost, only to find, to his dismay, that he obviously was a fool and knave for he saw nothing on the looms. On the day set for the grand parade, the knavish philosophers collected their royal fee, dressed the emperor in his pot-bellied nakedness, and skipped out of town as the parade began. The whole populace joined the courtiers in praising the king's garments, none daring to admit that they saw nothing but the emperor's nudity, lest they be branded as self-admitted fools and knaves. The entire parade of folly collapsed, as the shame of king and people was exposed by a child's honest remark, "The emperor has no clothes!"

This story has often been retold, with no small homilies on the feelings of king and people. But, significantly, the boy has been neglected, as truth usually is. Consider the future of that boy: with one small truth he exposed a national and personal lie. With a grain of truth, he turned a people's glory into shame. It is no wonder nothing is said of him. The knavish philosophers got off scot free, and rich as well. Emperor and people went on with their everyday activities, eating, drinking, marrying and giving in marriage. But the small boy was to old age an outcast: he had told the truth and shamed his race. Not only the king's nakedness, but that of his people, even of his father and mother, had been exposed to the public gaze by his truth. None were consciously naked until his truth destroyed their lie, ripping away their fig-leaf of common hypocrisy. The boy went on speaking the truth. Everyone knew him, but few dared hear him, since few desired to be naked again.

Now this story has a modern parallel in the life and work of the philosopher of religion, Cornelius Van Til, who, like the boy of old, looked at the reigning philosophy and declared, "The emperor has no clothes!" Of perhaps no other contemporary thinker can it be said that

16

he is both as well known and as little read as Van Til. The reaction of reviewers and readers to the publication in his *New Modernism, An Appraisal of the Theology of Barth and Brunner*, in 1946, was an occasion of outraged shock and horror, one of such dimensions as to make significant reading from this short distance. The book was an unspeakable offense, an outrage, a desecration of all philosophy and theology. The ostensibly orthodox *Calvin Forum*, a few years later, in discussing Van Til's philosophy, did so with such intemperate heat and language that its death was precipitated. Here, apparently, was an Ishmael, whose hand was raised against every man. Or was it not the reverse, with every man's hand raised against Van Til?

Why the reason for all this passion? What is it in his thinking that militates all contemporary theologies and philosophies against him?

To understand this, we must first of all look again at the Bible itself, rather than to the Graf-Wellhausen rescension of it. According to that document, the temptation of man was to "be as God, knowing good and evil" (Gen. 3:5 RV), that is, man was to be his own god, determining what constitutes good and evil according to the dictates of his own nature. To this temptation, man submitted, and in terms of this concept man lives. Here, then, is the origin of the concept of autonomous man, who is the point of departure in philosophy, whose thinking is creative, and whose reason has the right of judicial review over all of creation and its Creator. Here too is the point of origin of most theology and philosophy, in man the knower, the determiner of categories of thought, who tolerates God only if all notions of antecedent being are first of all dispensed with. This autonomous man will tolerate God only if direct revelation is eliminated, if the simple identification of Scripture with the Word of God is dropped, and God's relation to man made paradoxical or dialectical. Thus, it is not God who is known directly, but man's own consciousness. It is not God who speaks simply, but again man's own reason. God is either eliminated from the scene, or allowed to co-exist with autonomous man on man's own terms.

Let us again return to the naked emperor and his hypocritical courtiers and populace. When the honest lad's remark was made, that emperor was exposed in all his bulgy and bloated nakedness, and his worshipping followers revealed as fools and knaves. Thus, everyone's pride was hurt, and everyone's shame exposed. The animosity of all was directed therefore against the lad. But a direct attack was impossible: it would be too revelatory of their knavery. As a result, the court

17

hangers-on insisted that they agreed with the lad's emphasis on truth but rejected his methodology. "We are as much concerned with seeing the nature of reality as this young man," they insisted, "but we cannot tolerate this radical and disgraceful methodology." Much more would have been accomplished, if instead of saying, 'The emperor has no clothes,' he said, 'The emperor has no overcoat,' and had even offered to provide him one. This would have established common ground between them instead of destroying it. The boy, it was agreed, was an extremist who had destroyed his case and eliminated any standing ground by making it clear that the emperor had in fact *forsaken* clothing instead of politely remarking that the emperor had *some* clothes.

This has been the charge levelled also against Van Til. His philosophy leaves nothing to the *consistent* natural man. The religious hangers-on of autonomous man and his philosophy are insistent that their emperor be allowed all but his overcoat, that natural man be allowed valid knowledge of everything except God and matters pertaining to revelation. Fundamental to this assumption is the belief in an area of neutral facts which are equally available to God and man and derive their meaning from themselves. This belief, destructive of all thinking, remains common to most religious philosophy, although it has been attacked from various sources of late, with differing emphases. Alan Richardson, for example, has written that "the illusion of 'objective' or uninterpreted history is finally swept away. The facts of history cannot be disentangled from the principles of interpretation by which alone they can be presented to us *as history*, that is, as a coherent and connected series or order of events. Christian faith supplies the necessary principle of interpretation by which the facts of the biblical and Christian history can be rationally seen and understood."[1] Facts and interpretation are inseparable. The neo-orthodox and existentialist answer to this problem is to eliminate the old subjective-objective relationship, and its static conception of objective being and to replace it with the divine-human encounter, with the transcendental philosophy of pure act. Neither facts nor God have any meaning in themselves but only in terms of this interaction: man's experience of this encounter is the final point of reference in all interpretation. But, according to Van Til, "in the Christian view of things it is the self-contained God who is the final point of reference . . . For the Christian, facts are what they are, in the last analysis, by virtue of the place they take in the plan of God."[2] The natural man, the subject of the naked emperor, has a very definite bias in his thinking but is insistent that the young man alone is biased. Van Til is emphatic on the fallacy of all attempts to establish a principle of interpretation other than God. If, after the fashion of Thomas Aquinas and Bishop Butler, we establish a neutral principle of coherence or rationality, or like Clark and Carnell, enthrone the law of contradiction, two major concessions are involved. First, we reason from man's principle to God and enthrone our law over God as basic to all human and divine process. If the law or principle is the basic tool for understanding, then it and not God is basic to thinking, to interpretation. But if God is the Creator, then God Himself is the only true principle of interpretation. Second, this approach "allows that the natural man has the plenary ability to interpret certain facts correctly even though he wears the colored spectacles of the covenant-breaker. As though covenant-breakers had no axe to grind. As though they were not anxious to keep from seeing the facts for what they really are."[3] Increasingly, the history of philosophy is making it obvious that all philosophy now has either a reference point in man as ultimate, or in God as ultimate. It is apparent also that if the Scripture is right in asserting that "the heavens declare the glory of God; and the firmament sheweth his handywork" (Ps. 19:1), then every fact in creation witnesses to man concerning God. Man thus is not in a world with a neutral witness nor is he himself a neutral observer. If he fails to acknowledge this witness of creation it is because he deliberately suppresses that witness. And since he himself is a created being, he suppresses also the witness of his own nature and arrogates to himself an independent principle of interpretation, one in which he becomes his own god. Instead of recognizing that he is created, man assumes that he is ultimate; as such, he refuses to tolerate an independent and ultimate being such as God: God can at best exist only as another god among gods, with a senior status perhaps, but an unquestionably emeritus rank.

But if God has truly and causally created all things, is self-contained and sovereign and by his providence governs and controls all things, then no fact is a fact apart from God and has a full and valid interpretation apart *from Him*. Every fact is a God-created and God-interpreted fact and this world exists only as a God-created and God-interpreted world. While man's knowledge of the world, and of Scripture, cannot be exhaustive, yet it can be true to the measure that it recognizes and interprets what has been fully interpreted by God. In principle, therefore, autonomous man is incapable of any true knowledge if he be faithful to himself as the sole principle of interpretation,

19

but because "man is not a finished product,"[4] he does not manifest this total collapse in this life. This radical incapacity of the consistent natural man is in every realm of knowledge and every aspect of reality. His failure is not limited to the field of religion but is equally applicable to natural science. If all facts are God-given facts, then all facts have a common source of interpretation, and to reject it in one area is to reject it in all. Man is rescued from this extremity only by his failure to be consistent to himself; he thinks theistically where he can safely do so, while rejecting the ground of his knowledge, Autonomous man is thus like some Western families, whose sole means of subsistence is in swinging a wide rope. Such men emphatically deny that they rustle cattle, although they have no other visible means of support, while at the same time living entirely on the ranchers' stock. Thus natural man does have knowledge, but it is borrowed knowledge, stolen from the Christian-theistic pasture or range, yet natural man has no knowledge, because in terms of his principle the ultimacy of his thinking, he can have none, and the knowledge he possesses is not truly his own. If the rustler were faithful to his profession of honesty, he would either starve from lack of food or be compelled to honesty. If the natural man were faithful to his own presuppositions, he would either admit that he has no knowledge whatsoever and can know nothing, or he would turn to the ontological trinity as the sole source of knowledge and only true principle of interpretation. The natural man has valid knowledge only as a thief possesses goods.

For Van Til to say of autonomous man that "the emperor has no clothes" is thus offensive; his critics would insist that he merely say, "The emperor has no overcoat." In other words, in abandoning the self-contained God, autonomous man has merely discarded a heavy overcoat but is still fully clothed, and, in terms of summer weather, properly dressed. But Van Til is insistent that autonomous man in discarding God has discarded everything, and, if consistent to his principle, has no valid knowledge of anything, including himself, for he also is a God-created and hence God-interpreted fact. The emperor and his followers became involved in their disgraceful predicament precisely because they refused to know themselves. By virtue of the fall, men are sinners before God, a fact they are unwilling to acknowledge. The knavish philosopher-weavers exploited this wilful blindness on the part of the emperor and people and hence led them to rob themselves and to parade into shame. And this is Van Til's challenge to them, to face the fact that they are nothing more than sinning creatures living in a God-created world explicable only on God's terms and his interpretation. The champions of autonomous man accuse Van Til of using a faulty methodology to establish a truth they ostensibly welcome with him, when in actuality the question of methodology is an evasion of the basic truth, namely, the nakedness of autonomous man and his refusal to acknowledge his nakedness.

The emperor had no clothes but did not dare admit it. As he paraded down the street, he felt the sun on his bare back, and the light breeze on his naked shanks, and he knew that he was fully exposed, whatever the sycophants said concerning his magnificent robes. In like fashion the natural man knows his nakedness. Adam and Eve, being naive and still young in deceit, hid themselves, saying, "I was afraid, because I was naked; and I hid myself" (Gen. 3:10). Their descendants, more hardened in revolt, are not so honest. They parade openly, claiming to be dressed with the very garment of God, with royal garb, emperor's clothes. They do so by a metaphysics of correlativity between God and man, as Van Til has pointed out in his analysis of Reinhold Niebuhr.[5] They begin with an anti-metaphysical bias; they cannot tolerate nor are interested in God in Himself, in the ontological trinity. Man and God are alike involved in history; God is not above and beyond it as the sovereign Creator. To give God this sovereign status reduces Christian faith to metaphysical truths instead of an existential relationship in which the individual finds true particularity and true universality in himself and becomes his own principle of interpretation. Man and God are both involved in the universe, which is the ultimate reality. Man's original sin is not an ethical act but a metaphysical fact created by the time-eternity, finite-infinite antithesis and tension. Because the fall was not an historical act in the field of ethics but is a metaphysical fact concerning man, ethics disappears into a dubious metaphysics, and personal responsibility fades away to be replaced by an involved universe whose development as a social context is the basic reality. Thus history becomes the primary concern, rather than God, or human responsibility.

Man's role in this picture is more clearly stated by Barth, concerning whom Van Til writes:

Feisser is no doubt formally correct when he says that according to Barth we must start with God's revelation in Christ. God is for Barth identical with his revelation to himself in Christ. The God and the man of Barth become what they are because of their common relation to Christ. They *become* what they are in Christ; they are what they are because of a common *Geschichte*. Man *participates* in the history of Christ. He exists to the extent that he participates in this history.

And this history is the history of redemption. Man exists to the extent that he participates in Christ's redemptive work for all and every man. Man exists to the extent that he is the co-redemptor with Christ of mankind.[6]

Not God in Himself, but God in his relationship is the emphasis, and God is exhaustive in his relationship. And man always participates in the life and history of God, as well as in His being. As a result, the nakedness of man is covered with garments stolen from God. But the God whom man creates thus to clothe himself, is not the God of Scripture, nor a God who has being in Himself. He is only an existential relationship. As Brunner has stated it in *The Philosophy of Religion*, "For our knowledge, the Absolute is no more—though also no less—than a necessary limiting conception."[7] God is not a self-existent God. But when God ceases to be God, man also ceases to be man. Without a self-existent God from whence we derive meaning and the principle of interpretation, man finds himself naked; his borrowed clothes are as non-existent as his God of dialectics. His only reality becomes a meaningless universe of brute factuality. The one philosopher who faced more or less frankly the nakedness of the natural man was Nietzsche, who dispensed entirely with the attempt to borrow from God. As a result, he faced nihilism. Every attempt to give meaning became purely his own truth and had no meaning apart from himself. Believing God dead, he destroyed in turn every meaning he himself attempted to establish, recognizing that no God means no meaning, not even life. His insanity was the outcome of his philosophy; the antithesis was between cosmic meaning and completely personal meaning, between Christ, the principle of divine interpretation, and Antichrist, the negation of meaning, between Dionysius, the affirmation of self as meaning against all meaning, and the Crucified, the interpreter and the Word. The choice is clear cut; no God, no man; no God, no meaning. The natural man is naked in himself, and his borrowed and stolen garments cannot bear investigation. He has nothing in and of himself.

He insists, however, that he is clothed, and that he himself is the principle of interpretation, that nothing can be allowed "that is not in principle penetrable to the human mind . . . This idea of the essential penetrability to the human mind of any reality that we are to admit as having determinative significance for our lives implies that we, as human beings, are to be our own ultimate judges." This is the position of modern idealism, which, like neo-orthodoxy, has a finite God, who, like man, faces brute facts, the ultimately mysterious universe. Man and God are in the same predicament; they alike struggle to understand

and deal with reality. God is only "a principle of rationality within the universe." But "if the facts which face man are already interpreted by God man need not and cannot face them as brute facts. If the facts which man faces are really God-interpreted facts, man's interpretation will have to be in the last analysis a re-interpretation of God's interpretation."[8] Contemporary philosophy follows the lead of Kant, who ascribed "ultimate definitory power of the mind of man. Christianity, on the other hand, ascribes ultimate definitory power to the mind of man. What Eddington ascribes to man, the power of exhaustive dialectification of significant reality, Christianity ascribes to God."[9]

Van Til's purpose thus is to drive home the basic issue and to make both Christian and non-Christian aware of their presuppositions and to make them epistemologically self-conscious, to make them aware of how they know and what they know. Men are either covenant-keepers or covenant-breakers, either interpreting creation in terms of its meaning as established by the Creator, or attempting a false interpretation with filched odds and ends of material. No valid epistemology or theory of knowledge can begin elsewhere than with the ontological trinity, the absolute person, the concrete universal, the source of all meaning and interpretation. For Van Til, apologetics has a central importance and a renewed one, in that the non-Christian and inconsistently Christian systems and philosophies are exposed and corrected in terms of their nakedness. Thus Van Til's writings constitute a devastating and running attack on all contemporary systems in terms of his basic philosophy.

For Van Til, philosophy and history, universals and facts, are correlated in an important manner. Without God, there is no factuality or meaning. Before the facts can be approached, there must be the concrete universal, the ontological trinity; "in other words, only *theistic* facts are possible. We definitely maintain that for any fact to be a fact at all, it must be a theistic fact."[10] Van Til's approach is opposed to both the deductive and inductive methods. The deductive method begins with the ultimacy of certain axioms, not with God. The inductive method assumes that any kind of fact exists, rather than theistic facts. Van Til's approach is neither inductive or deductive, apriori or aposteriori, as these terms are historically understood, because "they contemplate man's activity in the universe but do not figure with the significance of God above the universe."[11] It is the firm conviction of every epistemologically self-conscious Christian-theist that no human being can utter a single syllable, whether in negation or in affirmation, unless it were for God's existence. Thus the transcendental argument seeks to discover what sort of foundations the house of human knowledge must have, in order to be what it is."[12]

The charge levelled against the consistent Christian philosopher is that he is guilty of circular reasoning, that he reasons from God to God, or from Scripture to Scripture. He ostensibly commits intellectual suicide because he says that he believes the Bible because it is true, and believes something to be true because it is in the Bible. According to Van Til,

> We hold it to be true that circular reasoning is the only reasoning that is possible to finite man. The method of implication as outlined above is circular reasoning. Or we may call it spiral reasoning. We must go round and round a thing to see more of its dimensions and to know more about it, in general, unless we are larger than that which we are investigating. Unless we are larger than God we cannot reason about Him by any other way, than by a transcendental or circular argument. The refusal to admit the necessity of circular reasoning is itself an evident token of Antitheism. Reasoning in a vicious circle is the only alternative to reasoning in a circle.[13]

All reasoning is either from God to God-given and God-interpreted facts, or from man to man-made interpretations of brute factuality. All reasoning is circular, but man refuses to admit to the circularity of his reasoning because he assumes that an infinite and exhaustive view of things is possible to himself, that he can, in other words, reason like God rather than as man.

Van Til's analyses of the history of philosophy are significant in their development of the epistemological presuppositions of the various schools. Greek philosophy he finds particularly important in that it represented the development of the antitheistic mind without any intermixture of Christian elements. Greek thinking lacked any true theistic elements, and, despite many references to God, believed basically in the self-contained and ultimate character of nature. God and man, form and content, spirit and matter, were essentially aspects of nature or identifiable with nature. It was not only possible to study the objective world without any reference to a God beyond the universe but possible to study God in the same manner also. Basically, man defined God, not God man. The human mind was capable of knowing any and all finite facts without any reference to God. The universe was ultimate, and the mind in a sense ultimate as part of that universe. Greek speculation assumed, first, that "all things are at bottom one." Second, the world of becoming is ultimate, whereas for Christian thought "Being is before becoming and independent of becoming."

2/451

Third, for Greek thought not only is change taken for granted as ultimate, but the many generated from the one is always identical with the one.[14] Greek thought, moreover, assumed the possibility of neutrality, whereas for Van Til the existence of an absolute God, from whom every creature has derived existence and to whom all are responsible, rules out all possibility of neutrality. The Greek mind is the end result of Eve's course.

Before Eve could listen to the tempter she had to take for granted that the devil was perhaps a person who knew as much about reality as God knew about it . . . That is, Eve was obliged to postulate an ultimate epistemological pluralism before she could even proceed to consider the proposition made to her by the devil. Or, otherwise expressed, Eve was compelled to assume the equal ultimacy of the mind of God, the devil, and herself. And this surely excludes the exclusive ultimacy of God. This therefore was a denial of God's absoluteness epistemologically. *Thus neutrality was based upon negation.* Or we may as well say that *neutrality is negation* . . . In connection with this we may remark in passing that when Eve listened to the tempter, she not only had to posit an original *epistemological pluralism,* but also an *original metaphysical pluralism.* She had to take for granted that a time created being could reasonably consider herself to be sufficiently ultimate in her being, as to warrant an action that was contrary to the will of an eternal being. That is, she had to equalize time and eternity not only, but she had to put time above eternity. It was in time that Satan told her the issue was to be settled. He said that it still remained to be seen whether God's threats would come true. The experimental method was to be employed. Only time could tell. Now this attitude implied that God was no more than a finite God. If He were thought of as absolute, it would be worse than folly for a creature of time to try out the interpretation of God in the test-tube of time. If He were thought of as eternal, such an understanding was doomed to failure, because in that case history could be nothing but the expression of God's will.[15]

Greek epistemology was Eve's thinking hardened into certainty.

In Greek thinking, as in Plato's, for example, time and eternity are very nearly identified, though at first they seem to be radically opposed to one another. Time is "the moving image of eternity"; the temporal and eternal are alike aspects of one general reality. Man is the temporal appearance of the eternal. As such, mankind and not the Second Person of the Trinity, Jesus Christ, is the mediator and interpreter. Time and eternity, moreover, are intermixed in mankind, whereas in Christ the two natures are without intermixture. For Platonism, philosophy ends in final mystery, whereas in Christianity the absolutely self-conscious God knows no mystery.

Plato's final mystery comes close to destroying all knowledge. Plato tried unsuccessfully with Heraclitus to find a basis for knowledge in the sense world alone. He tried unsuccessfully with Parmenides to find knowledge in the Ideal world alone. Because for Greek thought reality was at bottom one, and the entire universe ultimate, differentiation became virtually impossible. The Idea of the Good seemed to give a fundamental and underlying unity to knowledge, but since all other Ideas, including Ideas of mud, hair, filth, Ideas of evil, were equally ultimate and unchangeable, it posed a problem. A fundamental unity was assumed, but a fundamental diversity appeared. And if evil is as ultimate as good, there is then no underlying and controlling unity in the world of Ideas. Thus, no victory for any Idea was possible, and the only answer could be the compromise of all Ideas and the smoothing away of the significance of each. Moreover, it was not certain how these Ideas could even be known. How could the whole of any Idea be known in any sense object?

But if the Idea of the Good were thus cut up it could no longer furnish the unity that was indispensable for knowledge. In other words the doctrine of Idea left the problem of the one and the many and therefore that of creation unsolved. If the Ideal world was itself an ultimate plurality it could be of no service in an attempt to explain the plurality of the world we live in.[16]

The piece-meal apprehension of Ideas meant the end of knowledge also in an infinite regression. Nor could Plato escape this problem by making Ideas subjective, to be no more than our own thoughts, in which case knowledge would be reduced to illusion. Moreover, reality would then escape us, since most of reality would lie beyond the scope of man's knowledge and perception. Greek thought, as Van Til points out, was incapable of accounting for the fact of knowledge, and, by its philosophy tended to dissolve all knowledge into a common and meaningless reality. It could give no account of the world of experience but only tended to destroy it. The epistemology of Eve and her Greek sons, beginning with the equal ultimacy of God, the devil and man, ends with the equal irrelevancy and meaninglessness of all things. Every approach of Plato ended in failure. When he approached the problem of knowledge with an exclusively empirical, then with an exclusively metempirical, and finally with a union of the two methods, he failed to solve the dilemma. The three fundamental assumptions of Greek philosophy could not be overcome. First, all things remain at bottom one. Second, the many come out of the one, that is, the fact of change. Third, despite this becoming, all things remain at bottom one and differentiation becomes a problem. Thus, God, man and the devil were ultimately the same. The human and divine mind differ quantitatively rather than substantially.

26

In Augustine, the first principles of Greek thought were clearly and definitely rejected, according to Van Til, who regards Augustine as "a Christian-theistic philosopher with certain elements of Platonism in his thinking" but basically sound in the direction of his thought. For Augustine, the physical universe existed only as a creation of God. In his final outlook, "Augustine never separated his self-existence from God's existence." The universe is never the presupposition or basic reality for him; it is a creation of the absolute God. Accordingly, Augustine did not attempt to interpret reality in terms of Ideas but in terms of the ontological trinity, which "Furnished the basis of the principles of unity and diversity in human knowledge." Without the trinity, knowledge is impossible; here is plurality in unity, and the only means of escaping the dilemma of human knowledge, which resolves itself, on anti-theistic grounds, into either an ultimate plurality without unity or the possibility of knowledge, or an ultimate unity, without differentiation or meaning. In the triune God is the solution to this problem. But, because human knowledge is analogical rather than original or creative, it must always depend on divine knowledge.

Anything that a human being knows must first have been known to God. Anything a human being knows he knows only if he knows and because he knows God. For that reason too, man can never know anything as well and as exhaustively as God knows it. The fact that man's knowledge must always remain analogical is applicable to his knowledge of God as well as to his knowledge of the universe. God will never be understood in His essence by man. If He were, He would no longer be God. In that case there would be no solution for the problem of knowledge.[17]

This concept or doctrine of the trinity is the heart of Augustine's final epistemology and his radical disagreement with Greek thought. Plato, in assuming the ultimacy of the universe, could not escape the plurality of the world of the senses, because time and eternity were equally ultimate, and the Ideas and the senses likewise. Moreover, for Augustine, because true knowledge is analogical and involves thinking God's thoughts after Him, no one can have true intellectual knowledge of God unless he first has faith and accordingly is morally in tune with God. And since for Augustine the principle of evil was finite and that of good infinite, the unity of God's plan could not be broken and the categories of eternity are determinative for human thought.

In Scholastic philosophy the Aristotelian form of Greek thought triumphed finally over Augustinianism. The God of the Scholastics resembled closely the indifferentiated reality of the Greeks. This reality, analyzed into substance, structure and act, was called Father, Son and

Holy Ghost but bore scant resemblance to the ontological trinity of Augustine and Scripture. The Greek concept of the gradation of reality prevailed increasingly, and, as a result, for Scholasticism, salvation meant advancement on the scale of being. Evil (sin is metaphysical, not primarily ethical, and is low on the scale of being) is far away, removed from the center, thin in its participation in reality or being. Atonement in terms of this implied doing good, moralism, whereby one participated in the good and rose on the scale of being.

Because of this pagan element in Scholasticism, universals were a major problem. Universals and not the triune God provided the foundation for Scholastic thought, and nominalism was skepticism and despair as surely as the subjectivism of Ideas spelled trouble for the Greeks. They had no answer to the problem of the one and the many. Again there was no escape from the dilemma of ultimately undifferentiated and meaningless being as against an ultimate and unrelated pluralism. Scholasticism dealt with this problem by undercutting the Augustinian distinction between God and man with a Greek concept of being. Scholasticism thus sought to establish knowledge on a basis wherein no mystery existed for man, while mystery remained for God, whereas for the theist mystery exists for man but not for God. And, since history is determined by God, and time by eternity, it is not destructive of knowledge and meaning for mystery to exist for man. By setting up his own mind as the standard of truth, man destroys the possibility of truth. As Van Til has summarized it,

All the antinomies of human thought such as the relation of time and eternity, the one and the many, unity and diversity are involved in the problem of the universals. There are only two possible attitudes that can be taken to these antinomies. One can say that it is the business of the human mind to solve these antinomies and that unless it succeeds in doing so, there is no valid knowledge for man. Or one can say that since man is finite, it is clearly not the business of man to seek to solve these antinomies and that they must be solved in God or man's thought would be meaningless altogether. We may even go farther and say that antitheistic thought has *artificially created these antinomies*. If a man would say to himself that unless he can successfully climb the city hall he does not see how he can walk the street, we try to point him to the fact that the two accomplishments are not mutually dependent upon one another. Thus also it may not be necessary for man to be able to solve these antinomies of thought before he can have adequate knowledge for his life. We hold then that the Scholastics made the same mistake as the Greeks. They took for granted that words must be used either simply univocally or simply equivocally. They took for granted that every predicate used must apply to God in the same way that it applies to man or there can be no meaning in any predication at all.[18]

28

Although the Scholastics made reference to God in relation to the universals, nevertheless their solution was basically pagan. Seemingly, Scholasticism made faith important, in that the truths of revelation could be understood only by faith, and the natural world and its truths by the reason of natural man. In actuality, this was tantamount to a denial of the doctrine of creation, for the world was given a meaning inherent in itself and separate from God and hence discoverable by man apart from God and without reference to the fact of creation. Thus the universe was in effect cut loose from God and faith given only the area of mystery beyond the universe. But the Christian-theistic position asserts that apart from God nothing can be truly understood because all things are created by God and derive their meaning only from His sovereign will and creative purpose. It is not surprising, as Van Til has pointed out, that Roman Catholic thinking has been weak at this point in its doctrine of creation, and that such men as F. J. Sheen, in *God and Intelligence* are indifferent to the question of the eternity of the world and of matter.[19] Christian-theistic thinking is insistent upon "the complete self-consciousness of God and the consequent analogical reasoning on the part of man"[20] and makes the Bible central in its thinking. The fact of sin and man's rebellion against God and His interpretation of reality are basic to Christian epistemology, as is the fact of creation. Scholasticism, in believing that man can have true knowledge apart from God, forsakes the Christian-theistic view.

Lutheranism failed to make a full break with Rome, in that Luther attacked, not squarely the paganism present there, but the legalism that was its fruit. Luther tended to limit the image of God in man to the moral attributes of knowledge, righteousness and holiness. The Scholastic concept of the image was a *donum superadditum* to an already existing sense-world. Luther failed to stress sufficiently man's intellect and will in his view of the image. This broader conception of the image, as found in Calvin, means that all man's relationships as a self-conscious being are mediated to him through the image of God and hence are presented to him not only in terms of their created meaning, i.e., of God, but apprehended by him in terms of a created image which reflected the personality of God. To limit the scope of the image of God in man is to introduce impersonalism to the extent that we limit that image. As a result, Luther's early teaching on predestination, seemingly similar to Calvin's, differs from it by virtue of his impersonalism, which leads him to the fringes of philosophical determinism and a mechanical relationship between God and man. In like fashion, the means of grace, the Word and the sacraments, tend to work impersonally and to an extent mechanically, whereas no impersonalism between God and man can exist in a Christian-theistic epistemology. This led to the synergism of Melanchthon.

Synergism takes for granted that there can be no truly personal relations between God and man unless the absoluteness of God be denied in proportion that the freedom of man is maintained. Synergism assumed that an act of man cannot be truly personal unless such an act be unpersonal. By that we mean that according to synergism, a personal act of man cannot at the same time but in a different sense be a personal act of God. Synergism assumes that *either* man *or* God acts personally at a certain time, and at a certain place, but that they cannot act personally simultaneously at the same point of contact. In other words, synergism holds that personal activity on the part of man must always be at the expense of the personal character of that which surrounds him. Now this might seem to be an innocent matter as far as the universe around us is concerned. Yet the danger is very great since the depersonalisation involved does not limit itself to the material universe. It extends itself logically to God. And even if it does not at once and clearly oppose the personal activity of God, it remains a fact that there is always a tendency in synergism to hold on to some of the remnants of the Greek idea of a universe in some sense of the term, independent of God. If nowhere else the synergist at least extracts his own activity from the personal activity of God at some point of time. And just to that extent he has depersonalized God . . . The significance of Luther's conception of the image of God now begins to appear. The epistemological effect of it was that man's knowledge is once more made to depend in some measure upon something other than the personality and self-consciousness of God. There are elements of Platonic Rationalism in Lutheranism. The spectre of an independent sense world looms upon the horizon once more. Lutheranism has not learned to interpret all reality in exclusively eternal categories. Man is given originality at the expense of God.[21]

According to Van Til, evidence of this weakness in Lutheranism is further seen in the Lutheran conception of the Person of Christ. The two natures of Christ are seen as blending entirely, and both natures as present in the elements of the Lord's supper. According to Krauth, "To say that the nature of Christ is personally present without his humanity is to deny that his humanity is part of his personality and the doctrine of the incarnation, falls to the dust."[22] The orthodox formula of Chalcedon is thus virtually rejected, as is its declaration, directed against the Eutychian heresy of a single nature, which asserted the two natures "without confusion, without conversion or change." The Lutheran position leads to the assertion that the human can become the divine, that the eternal and the temporal can intermingle, that the two can have an independent or co-equal existence, that the eternal can be temporalized, and that the eternal is not determinative of the temporal. Scholasticism saw the weakness of man, not in his sin but in his finitude, not in ethics but in metaphysics, and Lutheranism at times tends to this same position. The Christian-theistic view is that unity and diversity, the one and the many, exist in equal ultimacy in the ontological trinity. The antitheistic view denies this and seeks the ultimacy of the one and many in the universe. When Scholasticism thus debated the question of universals, it had virtually abandoned the theistic view and sought its answer within the frame-work of the universe. Lutheranism, in seeking to some extent its principle of unity in an intermingling of the eternal and temporal, set forth in dramatic fashion in its concept of the Lord's supper, is refusing to accept the determinative character of the eternal and insisting that man's freedom is endangered if the temporal is not fused into the eternal. Such a view tends to deny reality to anything in eternity which does not at the same time exist in time, whereas the consistently theistic view holds that the only solution to time lies in eternity. The natural outcome of this intermingling is an insistence on the independence of man, because time is determinative of both the temporal and the eternal. The incarnate Christ becomes determinative of not only the Second Person of the Godhead but the trinity as a whole, because he works in time and the trinity in eternity. God must therefore limit Himself out of respect for His creatures; He cannot infringe on their independence, because time is the arena of ultimate reality, not eternity. Accordingly, the sinner determines his own salvation; God's grace starts or assists him to that end; it cannot determine him without destroying the meaning of time and its centrality. To grant the sinner this capability has far-reaching implications, as Van Til discerningly points out:

If one maintains that he can approach Christ of his own accord even though he is a sinner, he may as well say that he can approach the Father too. And if one can say that he knows what the fact of sin means without the enlightenment of the Holy Spirit, he may as well say that he can know other facts without reference to God. In fact he may as well say that he can know any and every fact without reference to God. If one fact can be known without reference to God there is no good reason to hold that not all facts can be known without reference to God. When the elephant of naturalism once has his nose in the door, he will not be satisfied till he is altogether in.[23]

Thus Lutheranism veers from an impersonal and mechanical determinism to an insistence on the independence of man. In neither extreme is the personal God fully determinative of time; the determination lies within the universe or within man. Despite its great beginnings, Lutheranism has been unwilling to follow the Reformation faith to its philosophical conclusions.

31

In Arminianism, as Van Til analyzes it, the unwillingness to face the full implications of original sin carried Protestantism further along on the road of concessions. In Watson, sin is ascribed to finitude rather than to moral revolt against God. Evil and finitude of necessity go together in this view, and man needs a savior not because of a moral condition but because he is a human being. In other words the implication is that man needs to be delivered not so much from sin as from creaturehood, from his finitude into infinitude. Moreover, from the Arminian point of view, man's rationality and freedom involve and include his ability to change the history God has planned, or to do things God has not planned. In short, man's life is outside the plan of God, constitutes a fact beyond God's control, one to which God can offer assistance but cannot govern. We are here on the road to the modern philosophic point of view which sees the spacetime continuum as the matrix of all reality. God exists, and is in the picture, but increasingly as a spectator; on the sidelines, ready to cheer man on but unable to determine the course and outcome of the race. Arminianism allows God and Christ onto the scene only to start the race, remove certain obstacles, and to award a prize. The final determination of events belongs to man. Arminianism further holds that, to be truly ethical, the will of man must be exclusively responsible for what is done. But the measure of self-determination demanded for man is an impossibility, and a significant impossibility, in that such self-determination is possible for God alone. Since man is a creature, living in a created world, in time governed by God, his act cannot suddenly break context with its entire world. The act of a creature, in a created world and in created time, can be only a created act. It is not only a personal act and a responsible act, but also a created act. Thus, in its concept of the ethical act, Arminianism claims for man what is possible only with God and thereby robs God to honor man. Moreover, God is further robbed by making evil virtually mean finiteness. If evil is finiteness, and finitude is the inherent condition of man, then the Greek dilemma is again with us, namely, that evil is as ultimate as the good, that evil is a part of the ultimate reality. Primacy is given to the temporal realm, which is the determinative one in this view, and evil is made basic to the temporal realm because finitude is inherent in it. The moral evil of Christian thought is eliminated; man is too independent for a concept of transmitted original sin to be credible. Theology thus gives way to an anthropology and God to man, eternity to time.

In Calvinism the Greek element was eliminated from Christian theistic thought and a consistent epistemology formulated. The false independence of man was shown for what it is, and the noetic influence of sin fully recognized. Scripture was made central to thinking, and the work of the Holy Spirit in the restoration to man to the true knowledge of God emphasized. Calvin's conception distinguished between the narrower and wider sense or understanding of the image. In the narrower sense, it applies to the true knowledge, true righteousness, and true holiness which man possessed when created by God. The fall destroyed this image, whereas the image in its broader sense, man's rationality and morality, his intellectual and emotional life, remain still in God's image, but with limitations. Man retains these aspects of his nature, but in a blinded sense. He is rational, but his rationality is spiritually blind, emotionally distorted, and out of kilter in terms of its created purpose, i.e., to function analogically, to think God's thoughts after Him and to interpret and experience life in terms of the will of God. Man, while spiritually blind, is still a person, and therefore the synergism of Luther is no necessity for Calvin. Synergism faced an either-or situation; either God acted, or man acted; it did not dare face the ultimate question, either God is a person or man is a person. For Calvin, man is a personality because God is a person. The sinner, a created person, cannot know God aright unless new light is given him by the Scripture, and the power of sight restored by the Holy Spirit working in his heart. Salvation is not the eternalization of man but rather his restoration to his original perfection and a development thereof. The incarnation is therefore not made necessary by man's finitude but by his sin. Since man's finitude is not the problem, Christ's human nature in the Lutheran sense is not needed in the sacrament. The eternal order is the determinative one, and God saves man *in* time, not *because* of time. God saves man *through* the incarnation, by means of the appearance of the Second Person of the trinity in history and his incarnation, whereby human nature was united without intermingling with the divine nature. The incarnation was the *means* of salvation, but the *cause* of salvation was to be found only in the foreordained and predestinated eternal counsel of God, only in the ontological trinity. To emphasize the incarnation, and especially the human nature of Christ, as against the ontological trinity, is to insist on mixing the temporal and eternal and shifting the area of reality away from the eternal and from God. As Van Til has stated it, "it is upon the development of these teachings of Calvin that we must depend for a consistent Christian epistemology. Calvin did not mix the categories of the temporal and eternal. He did not succumb to the temptation of giving man a false independence in the work of salvation. Hence he alone of all the Reformers could rid himself of the last remnants of Platonic reasoning."[24]

Two significant aspects of Calvin's theology point up the nature of his Christian theistic thinking; these are his doctrine of covenant theology and the trinity. In Calvinism, there is no subordinationism in the doctrine of the trinity. The persons of the trinity are representationally exhaustive of one another and represent the solution, on the eternal level, of the one and many principle. Because the persons of the trinity have an equal ultimacy, the principles of unity and diversity have an equal ultimacy. As Van Til analyzes it,

This mutual exhaustion of the persons of the trinity places one before the choice of interpreting reality in exclusively temporal categories or in exclusively eternal categories. The demand of the doctrine of the trinity when thus conceived is that reality be interpreted in exclusively eternal categories inasmuch as the source of diversity lies in the trinity itself and could never be found in a sense world beyond God. Hence the problem of the one and the many, of the universal and the particular, of being and becoming, of analytical and synthetic reasoning, of the apriori and the aposteriori must be solved by an exclusive reference to the trinity. The only alternative to this is to assume responsibility for trying to explain the whole of reality in temporal terms. Thus man is placed before a clear alternative and there is no longer a temptation to attempt a solution of those problems by seeking intermixtures of the temporal and the eternal.[25]

On this concept of the trinity, Calvin established his covenant theology. Since the persons of the trinity are representationally exhaustive of one another, it follows that human thinking is representational also. Since God is the creator and determiner of all things, and since all persons, things and acts are created facts, truly understandable only in terms of the ontological trinity, it follows therefore that in every fact and in any fact, man is face to face with God. Nothing exists in a neutral or impersonal world; all things exist in a created world in which every fact is surrounded by the personality of God.

Even the meeting of one finite personality with another finite personality would not be truly personal if there were an impersonal atmosphere surrounding either or both of these personalities. What makes their meeting completely personal is the fact the personality of each and of both is surrounded by the personality of God. Hence all personal relationship between finite persons must be mediated through the central personality of God. Every act of a finite person must in the nature of the case be representational *because the only alternative to this is that it should be completely impersonal.* We may even say that every act of the infinite personality of God must be representational because the only alternative to it would be that it would be impersonal. The trinity exists necessarily in the manner that it does. We have seen this to be so because the principles of unity

34

and diversity must be equally original. Accordingly, when we come to the question of the nature of finite personality it is not a handicap to finite personality to think of itself as related in some way to the personality of God, but that it is the very condition of its existence. A finite personality could function in none other than a completely personalistic atmosphere, and such an atmosphere can be supplied by him only if his existence depends entirely upon the exhaustive personality of God. It is in this manner that Calvin conceives of the personality of man. Man is not a metaphysically independent being. . . . Calvin is very sure that unless man were operating within God's plan, man would not be operating at all. It is not with apologies that Calvin proposes his doctrine of the will of man, but he sets it forth boldly as the only alternative to complete impersonalism. Calvin was keenly conscious of the fact that *the covenant theology furnishes the only completely personalistic interpretation of reality.* The false striving of Lutheranism and Arminianism for a personal act that should be unipersonal in the sense of not being surrounded by a completely personalistic atmosphere, Calvin is convinced, would lead, if carried out consistently, to the rejection of the whole Christian-theistic scheme of thought.[26]

For Calvin, man's true knowledge of himself and his knowledge of God came simultaneously. Since all knowledge is derived from analogical thinking on the basis of the revelation of God in Scripture, and since all meaning is derived from God, true self-knowledge comes only as God is known. Thus the traditional proofs of God meant little to Calvin, in that they assumed that on the basis of prior true knowledge, man advanced to the final knowledge, of the existence of God. The arguments assume the neutrality of the mind, whereas Calvin was convinced of the enmity of the mind and man against God. Moreover, the proofs of God first assumed the independence of the mind of man and of natural facts from God and thereby conceded to the opposition rather than advanced the theistic cause. Calvin's doctrine of God does justice to both transcendence and immanence, while giving priority to transcendence. God's nature and will are never separated; His will is always expressive of His nature, and, as a result, His activities are always completely personal. His insistence on the aseity of the Son is basic to his doctrine of the trinity: no subordinationism is tolerated. The significance of this Van Til has emphasized:

If there is any subordinationism it implies that God is to that extent no longer the sole interpretative category of all reality. The measure of subordinationism that any system of theology retains in its doctrine of the trinity is indicative of the measure of paganism in such a theology. Plato's independent sense world looms upon the horizon the moment subordinationism is given any place.[27]

In the modern era, the question of epistemology has come to the foreground in philosophy. Ostensibly, this is a by-passing of metaphysics and an elimination of God from philosophy as irrelevant. Actually, the full significance of the Christian theistic position is most clearly seen in the extent to which modern philosophy goes to eliminate an independent and sovereign God. The issues are more sharply drawn therefore between the consciousness of man and the consciousness of God as the frame of reference.

In Descartes, the ground of all certainty is the human consciousness in independence not only from the universe around him but especially from God. For Calvin the personality of man cannot be known nor can exist without the personality of God. For Descartes, nothing can be known without man's self-consciousness and personality in itself. The universe is a mechanistic one, and God merely the creator of the machine, now functioning in independence of Him. The machine has its own laws and workings, and the inventor need not be known in order to understand the machine. The lives of the Wright brothers are of great interest to any student of the history of aviation, but utterly irrelevant to any understanding of the principles of flight or to the piloting of aircraft today. The Wright brothers created the first successful plane, but they did not create the principles of flight which made that plane possible; they merely used them. The God of Descartes is ultimately in the same position. More than that, man rather than God is made the ultimate source of universal laws and interpretation.

As a result of Descartes' point of departure, two lines of thought developed in philosophy, empiricism and rationalism. Empiricism holds that the individual man is the standard of truth and holds to the ultimacy of the sense world. The universals are purely subjective. The climax of such thought was the skepticism of Hume, for whom no knowledge was possible. Rationalism sought to interpret reality in terms of certain apriori principles. These apriori principles, however, were not anchored in the ontological trinity or in eternity but in the human mind as ultimate. In Spinoza and Leibniz rationalism reached its climax. For Spinoza, God, man and the universe are but individuations and aspects of the general Idea of substance. But, as Van Til has pointed out, to say that all is God is no different than saying nothing is God. "Univocal reasoning must always lead to negation. Univocal reasoning is based upon negation. The very presupposition of univocal reasoning is that there is no absolute God. If there were an absolute God it is ipso facto out of the question to apply the categories of thought to Him in the same way that they are applied to man."28 Leibniz sought individuation on the basis of complete description and by reduction to mathematical formulae. Revelation was thus an impossibility. The interpreter is the mind of man, not the mind of God, and the mind of man can wholly comprehend all reality. The equal ultimacy of the one and many is sought without success in the universe, and the old theory of the gradation of being espoused. None of these devices enabled Leibniz to escape the dilemma of Spinoza or to rescue religion as he sought to do; having begun with the ultimacy of the universe, he could do more than attempt to analyze it into both God and man. "As Leibniz sought to be wholly univocal, so Hume sought to be wholly equivocal in his reasoning. As in the philosophy of Leibniz God lost his individuality in order to become wholly known, so in the philosophy of Hume God maintained his individuality but remained wholly unknown."[29]

Kant's solution to the question is a fusion of rationalism and empiricism. All rational and empirical data had disappeared and the human consciousness faced an undifferentiated reality dissolved either into unrelated sensations or faced as mysterious bulk. Kant's answer was not new: his radicalism was. Kant sought to save the objects, God and the world, by destroying the traditional conception of the subject-object relation and making autonomous man a macrocosm containing both God and the world. Because man was the interpreter, subjectivity, the old ghost haunting philosophy, was ostensibly banished. Even as for Christian thought, the self-consciousness of the sovereign God has no problem of subjectivity, in that it comprehends all things, having created and sustaining them, so in Kant subjectivity disappears only if it be granted that autonomous man replaces the ontological trinity and that in him being is exhausted in relation and that relation is exclusively internal. Philosophy previously had tended to fall into Kant's solution, but had regarded it as defeat; Kant accepted it as the means to victory.

To understand Kant's work, which was concerned with the problem of knowledge, it is necessary to see what he was contending against. Kant was concerned over the collapse of epistemology, over the reduction of knowledge to illusion in contemporary philosophy. He was thus attacking and superseding both empiricism and rationalism, empiricism for its acceptance of the validity of sensations as the source of all knowledge, and rationalism for its acceptance of innate ideas as needing no matter outside themselves. The unhappy outcome of both schools was a wretched dualism between mind and matter, between the knower and brute factuality, the physical universe, with no means of bridging the gap or establishing the validity of either sensations or

37

reason. Kant's concern was epistemology, not metaphysics, not what is real, but what can we know. Kant eliminated from consideration the old approach as dogmatic, since it merely involved an attempt to trace ideas to their sources, either innate ideas or sensations, in both instances the self having an essentially negative role. For Kant the true approach is the transcendental or critical, the study of pure reason itself. Kant was concerned with establishing in reason that which had a universality beyond human experience while yet necessary to it, reliable and applicable to the world of things. This method is transcendental because it is necessary to all experience, not because it transcends it. The transcendental is rationally prior and hence indispensable to knowledge, and the critical method is the finding of this indispensable condition. As a result, for the old dualism of mind and matter, Kant substituted a threefold world of subjective states, phenomena, and things-in-themselves. The subjective area is no longer the domain of knowledge, but neither is the realm of things-in-themselves. Here is Kant's sharp break with the past. Things-in-themselves lie beyond us and so beyond all knowledge, unknown and unknowable. We cannot say what these things-in-themselves are, but we can say that they exist, because they are a necessary postulate to experience. These are Noumena, basic to the knowing process and therefore postulated, but beyond that their reality is neither to be affirmed or denied; such a judgment is not possible. The basic realm is that of human knowledge, "the world of phenomena" or experience. Phenomena are not things-in-themselves but things-for-us, reality as humanity experiences it and as it is interrelated. Thus the attempt to correlate mind and matter, the knower and reality, is dropped entirely; it is not the correlation which constitutes knowledge but the experience, the synthetic power of the mind, the unifying of human experience. Sensations give only raw material; synthesis produces knowledge. It is not the *result* of combining experiences that is knowledge as much as the act of combining them. Thus knowledge is constitutive, creative, interpretive, and the common ability of all humanity. While another order of beings might have a different power of synthesis and thus live in a radically different world than ours, yet the validity of knowledge is not thereby denied, because absolute reality is not the object of knowledge. Practically speaking, humanity can say, according to Kant, "The world is my representation." Such a suggestion hints to the pluralism which William James was subsequently to develop. Yet Kant also assumed, to explain this capacity for synthesis and creative thinking, a transcendental ego which is the postulate of all knowledge. It is the universal Self, not an object of knowledge but the virtual source of knowledge. The Self therefore is the basic reality and hence not an object of knowledge. The universe and God are not objects of knowledge either, but for a different reason, in that they are regulative principles and ideas and limiting concepts, basic to knowledge as such, and whose existence in themselves is not a question for knowledge and hence neither to be affirmed or denied. Their status is as adjuncts of the transcendental ego.

Thus while Kant attacked empiricism and rationalism, his basic attack was on the concept of the ontological trinity, the self-contained God. Empiricism and rationalism had collapsed in their attempt to sever knowledge from dependence on God, and hence Kant's hostility to them, because for Kant's thinking the severance was both basic and necessary. Ultimate reality is declared to be unknowable; we are surrounded by brute factuality of which we are the creative interpreters. Instead of trying to establish knowledge by relating mind and matter, Kant finds it in the world of experience, in the world of phenomena, in synthetc reason. While reality may or may not exist beyond man, it most certainly exists in man. The true self, the transcendental ego is at least part (and possibly all) of that basic reality and thus by nature is the valid interpreter. The solution of Satan and Eve becomes steadily more explicit; man seeks to solve "the problem of God" by becoming God in his own eyes. According to Van Til,

If Kant's position were to be retained both knowledge and faith would be destroyed. Knowledge and faith are not contradictories by complementaries. Kant did not make room for faith because he destroyed the God on whom alone faith is to be fixed. It is true of course, that Kant spoke of a God as possibly existing. This God, however, could not be more than a finite God since He at least did not or did not need to have original knowledge of the phenomenal world. Kant thought that man could get along without God in the matter of scientific knowledge. It is thus that the representational principle which we saw to be the heart of the Christian-theistic theory of knowledge is set aside. If man knows certain facts whether or not God knows those facts, as would be the case if the Kantian position were true . . . whatever sort of God may remain He is not the supreme interpretative category of human experience.[30]

Hereafter the notions of being, cause and purpose must stand for orderings we ourselves have made; they must never stand for anything that exists beyond the reach of our experience. Any God who wants to make himself known, it is now more clear than ever before, will have to do so by identifying himself exhaustively with his revelation. And any God who is so revealed, it is now more clear than ever before, will then have to be wholly hidden in pure possibility. Neither Plato nor Aristotle were entitled by the methods or reasoning they employed, to reach the Unconditioned. The Unconditioned cannot be rationally related to man. There is no doubt but that Kant was right in this claim. Plato and Aristotle no less than Kant assumed the autonomy of man. On such a basis man may reason univocally and reach a God who is virtually an extension of himself or he may reason equivocally and reach a God who has no contact with him at all. Nor will adding two zeros produce more than zero.[31]

When Kant said that man could have knowledge apart from God, he maintained thereby the self-sufficiency of the phenomenal world and of the self. And yet Kant could not make an absolute of the phenomenal world, because it is the world of time which is itself subjective. Neither could he say that man's reason was valid for another order of being or inclusive of all possibility. Thus neither the universe, the mind of man, or the phenomenal world gave man any absolute or any ground of validity for his knowledge. For Kant's arguments against Christian theism to be valid,

... they must really be valid for all possible existence and thus be inclusive of the future as well as of the past. In other words Kant needs an absolute in order to make his arguments effective. . . . Accordingly, it is fair to say that Kant had to presuppose the existence of God before he could disprove it. It is thus that Kant has slain univocal arguments for the existence of God by a univocal argument against such arguments and has at the same time killed all univocal reasoning by showing that *all univocal reasoning, including his own, presupposes analogical* reasoning. As Samson died when he slew his enemies, so Kant died when he slew his.[32]

The issues, as Van Til points out, have been greatly clarified as a result of Kant's work. Anti-theism is insistent on interpretating reality in exclusively temporal categories and in rejecting any distinction between divine and human thought. Reasoning must be univocal. The ontological trinity is absolutely rejected as destructive of all history and reason. Christian theistic thought looms more clearly as the enemy of both pragmatism and idealism, both of which develop Kant's creativity of thought in their respective directions.

It is clear from Van Til's analysis of the history of philosophy that the difference between Christian theism and anti-theism is not confined to the existence of God but to the whole field of knowledge. Instead of both sharing a common knowledge of the world and being in disagreement as to whether God exists, or can and need be known, we have instead a radical disagreement as to the nature of all knowledge.

Christian theism's fundamental contention is just this, that nothing whatever can be known unless God can be and is known. In whatever way we put the question then the important thing to note is this fundamental difference between theism and anti-theism on the question of epistemology. There is not a spot in heaven or on earth about which there is no dispute between the two opposing parties. And it is the point that can bear much emphasis again and again.[33]

40

It is this insistence that constitutes the originality of Van Til's insight as well as the offense of his position.

The struggle therefore is one that covers the whole field of knowledge. It is precisely this that must be recognized as the basic issue. It is the Christian-theistic conception that nothing can be truly known unless God can be and is known, and this discrepancy and disagreement between the contending philosophies is apparent as we consider the question of the object of knowledge.

The object of knowledge is anything that is considered a *fact*, and here again the difference is obvious. What is a fact? Facts can belong to the physical world, to the realm of psychology, economics, mathematics, and so on. But what is a fact? Each philosophy differs as to what constitutes a fact. The conception of the physical world and the facts thereof vary radically in Augustine, Spinoza, Hume, and Kant. The "facts" vary from philosophy to philosophy; they are precisely the point of difference, in that each begins with certain basic assumptions and presuppositions.

What our opponents mean by the existence of any 'fact' is existence *apart from God*. That they mean just this is indisputable for the reason that such *existence apart from God* is ipso facto predicated for all 'fact' except of the 'fact' of God if the 'fact' of God is called a question. For any one to call the existence of God in question he must at least exist and *possibly* exist apart from God. It appears then that the very connotation of the term existence is in question. The antitheist maintains that the term existence may be applied as a predicate to any 'fact' even if the 'fact' of God's existence is not a fact. On the other hand the Theist maintains that the term 'existence' cannot be applied intelligently to any 'fact' unless the 'fact' of God's existence is a fact. In other words the anti-theist assumes that we can begin by reasoning univocally while the Theist maintains that we cannot begin otherwise than by reasoning analogically.[34]

The denotation and connotation of any fact cannot be separated. Every fact is and is what it is and means what it means by virtue of its creation by and place in the total providence of God and is not truly known on any other grounds.

There are, Van Til points out, those who insist that it is intelligible to think of the non-existence of God but who at the same time insist that we cannot intelligently think of the non-existence of man and his world. Each begins with a reality, a basic fact, which he insists must be taken for granted. Van Til sees four positions as possible with regard to the question of existence and non-existence. First, we can believe it reasonable to doubt the existence of God but not intelligible to doubt the existence of the universe. Second, we can doubt the existence of both God and the universe as the only intelligible step.

41

Third, we can insist that it is not intelligble to doubt the existence of either God or the universe. Fourth, we may hold it possible to think intelligibly of the non-existence of the universe but impossible to doubt the existence of God. Of these four positions, only the last is consistent with theism, not because Christianity denies the existence of the universe, but because it cannot consider the universe as the ultimate reality and therefore the ground of all thought. Without God, nothing can exist, and therefore God alone is the starting point of all intelligible thinking.

A person's conception of what constitutes a fact is thus governed by his starting point. It is here necessary to distinguish with Van Til between an immediate and an ultimate starting point. He explains it by the analogy of a diving board. A diver, standing on the tip of a board and seeing nothing around him but water can state that the end of the board is his starting point in an immediate sense. But in an ultimate sense the foundation of the whole board is his starting point, and he cannot eliminate from his recognition of his situation all except the tip and the water. As Van Til insists, the question at issue in philosophy is "not that of the immediate starting point. All agree that the immediate starting point must be that of our everyday experience and the 'facts' that are most close at hand. But the exact charge we are making against so many Idealists as well as Pragmatists is that they are taking for granted certain temporal 'facts' not only as a temporary but as an ultimate starting point."[35] Similarly, the Bible is not to be used as a source book in biology or to replace a paleontological study in Africa. "The Bible does not claim to offer a rival theory that may or may not be true. It claims to have the truth about all facts."[36] It is not claimed that one should go to the Bible instead of to Africa; what is claimed is that without the God of the Bible and the revelation therein given no fact can be truly known, nor can its existence be even posited. The opponents of Christian-theism insist on taking for granted that specifically which they need to and cannot prove, the independence and ultimacy of the mind and of brute factuality. Moreover, all facts owe not only their existence but their denotation and connotation to God, and every fact exists and must be known, if it is truly known, as a Christian theistic fact. Without the light of Scripture, no fact can be truly known. Not only facts, but all nature and history exist in terms of eternal categories.

Christian thinkers like Augustine and especially Calvin have been ready to take the human self as the proximate starting point, while anti-theistic philosophy takes the self as an ultimate starting point. This latter emphasis has become more consistently pronounced. Moreover, modern philosophy is less concerned with the object of knowledge than with the subject of knowledge, and the self is assumed to be the ultimate subject of knowledge. But the very challenge of Christian theistic philosophy

. . . is that God is the ultimate subject of knowledge. Man is and can be a subject of knowledge in a derived sense because God is the subject of knowledge in an absolute sense. Theologically expressed we say that man's knowledge is true because man has been created in the image of God. And for this reason too there can be no dispute about the relative priority of the intellect and the feeling of man. Since the personality of God is a complete unity so also the personality of man is a unity.[37]

The charge against all anti-theistic thought is that it is subjective, in that it sets up human thought or consciousness as the ultimate standard of truth. Because its concept of truth is derived from the mind or from experience, modern philosophy leads inevitably to a complete relativism in epistemology and metaphysics. At times it frankly forsakes the quest for truth and certainty, but it never candidly admits that the logical alternative is total relativism. In liberal theology, the same relativism is latent or explicit, and what passes for theology is little more than anthropology, and experience is emphasized as against truth or as the essence of truth. The sources of liberal and neo-orthodox theology are to be found in three main schools of philosophy, first in pragmatism, which assumes the subjective validity of all religion irrespective of its object. Next are the naturalists who emphasize logic rather than time and reduce whatever God may be tolerated to a logical universal binding together equally ultimate particulars. Last we have the idealists for whom God is the absolute, but a significantly empty absolute, in that the difference between God and man, and time and eternity, is erased by embracing all in a common and ultimate reality. Thus all are equally ultimate and God is a part of the universe rather than its creator and sustainer. God and man are alike aspects of reality; therefore, God at best can function as an associate or elder brother, assisting man in the interpretation of a reality He did not create and must Himself struggle to understand. God becomes a logical necessity rather than creator. Man is as necessary to God as God to man (as witness the philosophy of Pringle Pattison). By a constant insistence on the correlativity of time and eternity, and God and man, idealism tries to gain for man and time a status in terms of ultimate reality. All are alike embraced in a common and ultimate reality.[38]

43

Not only is there a radical difference between Christian theistic thought and anti-theistic philosophy with regard to the starting point of knowledge, but also, as we have seen, over the question as to whether the existence of the object of knowledge can be taken for granted apart from God. Furthermore, in view of the sinful nature of man, the interpretation in terms of God must come through Scripture. Error is the result of sin, although not all error in logic is due to sin directly. Nevertheless, the mind of man is in rebellion against and in enmity to God and establishes itself as its own God and own principle of interpretation. Man seeks to think creatively rather than to think God's thoughts after Him. Evil is the result of man's rebellion against God and is not original or ultimate, and because it is not, evil cannot be predicated of God or considered ultimate. Prior to the fall, the world and man were good, and evil and error were introduced by man's rebellion. Man's fall was his attempt to become the original interpreter rather than the re-interpreter, to be the ultimate instead of the proximate source of knowledge. Prior to the fall, Van Til asserts, man acted as the re-interpreter, recognizing that since he derived his being wholly and completely from an absolute God, his every act therefore was based on a more original and fundamental act of God. Man now must be restored to a like position, forsaking his role of original interpretation for re-interpretation, recognizing moreover that his consciousness is only the proximate starting point for knowledge. But man the sinner virtually insists that his present fallen and abnormal condition is the normal one and is resentful of any suggestion of abnormal mentality. As Van Til has pointed out, in the country of the blind, the man with sight was called a wild visionary. For the Christian, however, the answer is an absolute God, an absolute Bible, and absolute regeneration. The creative act and thought must be God's alone. Nothing which hints of the correlativity of God and man, of eternity and time, can be permitted. By such correlativity, idealism seeks to rehabilitate history, but in making historical reality exist in independence of God, it destroys the sovereignty of God, and the meaning of history. Evil becomes as ultimate as the good, and history becomes an irreconcilable and meaningless conflict. History has meaning and purpose only when wholly, i.e., finally, determined by the personal and sovereign God. Man then moves in a personal and purposive world, and time has direction and meaning. Instead of an impersonal universe in which good and evil are equally ultimate, he moves in a completely personal universe in which his activities have meaning, good is ultimately triumphant and every fact is purposive in terms of a common and ultimate will. Man's re-interpretation is possible because of God's prior and absolute interpretation. History has meaning precisely because it is absolutely predestinated by God. Man's activity is not mechanically determined because he lives in a completely personal environment and moves in purposive and personal history. Only as the ethical alienation of man from God is removed, can man again act derivatively and constructively in the field of God's original constructive activity and re-establish the original metaphysical relationship. For Van Til, there is no underlying metaphysical separation of man from God but rather an ethical alienation, a divorce with all the bitterness and alienation which attends such a situation. Any other conception of God makes God no more than an elder brother, setting an example for man and assisting men in their common task of trying to make sense of a senseless universe which is the ultimate reality. For the Christian, the physical universe is explicable also in terms of the spiritual because both have a common origin and unity in God.

It follows from this that the spiritual can be truly though symbolically expressed by the images borrowed from the physical. It is this conception that underlies Jesus' use of parabolic teaching. The vine and the branches give metaphorical but truthful expression to the spiritual union between Jesus and his own because the physical is created for the purpose of giving expression to the spiritual. We find then that one must first pre-suppose the anti-theistic conception that nature is independent of God before one can urge the argument that symbolical language is necessarily to an extent untruthful.[39]

Not only is language robbed of content by the anti-theistic position, but man's salvation is made impossible. With any conception of autonomous man, salvation disappears. Man is not subject to the covenant and to federal representation in Christ, and hence the atonement can have no meaning for man, who becomes isolated in his autonomy and a world of brute factuality. At the same time, this autonomy of man destroys his individuality and personality, in that he becomes lost in an impersonal world of brute factuality. Reality being ultimately an undifferentiated mass and equally good and evil, humanity also is ultimately an undifferentiated mass, and mass man becomes a problem.

In considering the subject-subject relationship, the usual question is whether, under this Christian view, it is any use for the Christian-theist to reason with his opponents or to seek their understanding of the Christian view of things. Since regeneration is required, of what value is philosophy? To answer this, we must again consider the problem of knowledge. All objects of knowledge in time and space, having been created by God, to be truly known must be known in relation to God. As Van Til asserts, the universals of knowledge as well as the objects of knowledge have their source in God and their relationships are in terms of the plan of God. The anti-theist, however, not only begins with the facts or objects of knowledge as ultimate, but also regards the universals as ultimate, and neither has anything to do with God. No reference beyond the facts and universals is needed. If God exists, therefore, he can only be another fact, another object of knowledge, rather than the one supreme object of knowledge, the ultimate fact and the ultimate universal. With such a discrepancy between the two views, it is not surprising that each considers the other blind.

But, Van Til states, the subject-subject relationship is not a problem if the subjects are Christian, or if they are unregenerate. The clash comes between the two opposing groups. To answer this, Van Til feels that it must be noted first that the normal state of man is that his whole consciousness, intellect, will or emotion, was created to be completely re-interpretative. Second, the revelation of God, manifested everywhere in a wholly personal universe, comes to the whole consciousness of man. Since God is absolute, man is always accessible to Him and can never escape. His witness and truth. Man's alienation from God is ethical; it cannot alter his metaphysical dependence on God. Because man is thus wholly accessible to God and resides in and is part of a completely personal universe, it then follows that all creation is instrumental in terms of the divine plan, and our philosophy is also instrumental.

The Christian can effectively attack every ground the anti-theist stands on, because the anti-theist is constantly on alien and hostile ground. When he sets up his reason as judge, and appeals to the law of contradiction, he contradicts himself, in that his universe is one of chance and abstract possibility, and reason and the law of contradiction are thereby rendered invalid. When a Christian thinker like Carnell declares, "Bring on your revelation! Let them make peace with the law of contradiction and the facts of history, and they will deserve a rational man's assent,[40] he has set up rational man, regenerate and unregenerate, as the criterion and judge over God and His truth. A criterion above Christianity itself which derives from man establishes man's ultimacy and supremacy of mind.

On any but the Christian basis man, using this reason, is a product of Chance and the facts which he supposedly orders by the 'law of contradiction' are also products of Chance. Why should a 'law of contradiction' resting on Chance be better than a revolving door moving nothing out of nowhere into no place? Only on the pre-supposition that the self-contained God of Scripture controls all things, can man know himself or anything else. But on this pre-supposition the whole of his experience makes good sense. Thus a truly *Christian* philosophy is the only possible philosophy. Other philosophies are or should be called such by courtesy. Those who crucify reason while worhipping it, those who kill the facts as they gather them, ought not really to be called philosophers. Insisting upon 'reason' as the test of truth they have completely divorced the operation of 'reason' from the turmoil of fact. They cannot find coherence in anything on their principle. Fear, nothing but fear in the dark, remains. Aldous Huxley's latest novel 'Apes and Essence' pictures strikingly the inevitable result of a philosophy that is not definite Christian philosophy.[41]

For the theist, the possible is that which is according to the will and nature of the absolutely self-conscious God, and God alone is the source of the possible, whereas for anti-theism the possible is the source of God. Thus their concepts of possibility differ. The division between the two is not always clearly discernable because of *incidental* agreements. Because the non-regenerate, by virtue of common grace, have a kind of recognition "of what should though it is not," they come to an incidental agreement with the Christian. The agreement is incidental, Van Til demonstrates, because their consciousness gives other grounds for the 'fact' at hand. As Van Til has pointed out, the pragmatist agrees with the Christian in opposing murder, but for pragmatic and humanistic reasons, whereas for the Christian the real reason is a concept of justice which has its foundation in the nature of the sovereign God. It becomes apparent at once also that they differ in their concept of justice, and that their agreement is incidental, formal and abstract. Moreover, even this incidental agreement exists only with regard to things proximate rather than things ultimate. Thus it is imperative to recognize that two types of consciousness exist, and that we cannot talk about reason in the abstract. The consistently regenerate reason and the consistently unregenerate reason have fundamental presuppositions regarding the nature of reason and reality which cannot be reconciled. However, Van Til calls attention to a fundamental and general human consciousness which existed before the fall. Adam's consciousness was re-interpretative and his knowledge valid. Although the range of his knowledge could not be as comprehensive as God's, its validity did not rest on range, because he reasoned "in an atmosphere of revelation. His very mind with its laws was a revelation of God. Accordingly, he would reason analogically and not univocally. He would always be presupposing God in his every intellectual operation."[42] Although man is now fallen, and the unregenerate man ethically alienated from God, he can never become God as he seeks to be.

47

He can never in reality exert the independence he claims. He remains metaphysically dependent on God. As a result, his consciousness, even in rebellion cannot sever itself from God but retains a formal power of receptivity. Moreover, the ethical alienation is not yet complete in degree. As a result, the Christian can speak to the unregenerate. For Van Til, metaphysically, only one type of consciousness exists, one in dependence upon God; ethically, two types of consciousness exist. On the basis of the one fundamental metaphysical consciousness, the subject-subject relationship is possible and effective. The unregenerate must be told that the Christian-theist has the true conception of the law of contradiction, i.e.,

Only that is self-contradictory which is contradictory to the conception of the absolute self-consciousness of God. If there were in the trinity such a self-contradiction there would also be in the matter of God's relation to the world. But, since the trinity is the conception by which ultimate unity and diversity is brought into equal ultimacy, it is this conception of the trinity which makes *self-contradiction impossible for God and therefore also impossible for man*. Complete self-contradiction is possible only in hell and hell is itself a self-contradiction because it feeds eternally on the negation of an absolute affirmation. Accordingly, we must hold that the position of our opponent has in reality been reduced to contradiction when it is shown to be hopelessly opposed to the Christian-theistic concept of God. Yet in order to bring this argument as closely to the nonregenerate consciousness as we may we must seek to show that the non-theist is self-contradictory upon his own assumptions, as well as upon the assumption of the truth of theism and that he cannot even be self-contradictory upon a non-theistic basis since if he saw himself to be self-contradictory he would be self-contradictory no longer.

Now when this method of reasoning from the impossibility of the contrary is carried out, there is really nothing more to do. We realize that if we call to mind again that if once it is seen that the conception of God is necessary for the intelligible interpretation of any fact, it will be seen that this is necessary for all facts. If one really saw that it is necessary to have God in order to understand the grass that grows outside his window he would certainly come to a saving knowledge of Christ, and to the knowledge of the absolute authority of the Bible. . . . It is well to emphasize this fact because there are Fundamentalists who tend to throw over-board all epistemological and metaphysical investigation and say that they will limit their activities to preaching Christ. But we see that they are not really preaching Christ unless they are preaching Him for what He wants to be, namely, the Christ of cosmical significance. Nor can they even long retain the soteriological significance of Christ, if they forsake His cosmological significance. If one allows that certain facts may be truly known apart from God in Christ there is no telling where the limit will be.[43]

Every claim of the anti-theist must be challenged and revealed for what it is. The agnosticism of modern thinking claims a scientific humility and reserve in the face of the unknown. But in its very assertion of agnosticism it makes a tremendous statement about ultimate reality in that it excludes God as the ultimate fact and limits Him to the possibility of being a fact among facts. All man's thinking rests on a concept of ultimate reality, and agnosticism definitely excludes God as ultimate reality and allows Him only the possibility of correlatively and co-existence. To say that science makes no pronouncement about the ontological trinity is to ascribe to science a tremendous pronouncement, one which makes brute factuality the ultimate reality. A universal negative statement virtually is made with vast implications. Facts exist in a void, and nothing can be said about the void unless it is posited that some universals exist beyond the void. Thus agnosticism cannot argue for its position without assuming far more than its position allows. Basically, as Van Til shows, it assumes the truth of the Christian-theistic system in order to operate and assert itself. It is self-contradictory on Christian premises, and self-contradictory on its own premises unless theism is assumed to be true. The unbeliever is thus able to think and work only on the basis of a practical reason which presupposes the Christian frame of things. On his own premises, he can know nothing; on borrowed premises, he is able to think and work, but for all his results, he remains in the paradoxical position of the cattle rustler mentioned previously. He has no knowledge on the basis of his own principles; he has valid knowledge only as a thief possesses stolen goods. As Van Til bluntly states the issue,

The question is one of 'this or nothing.' The argument in favor of Christian theism must therefore seek to prove that if one is not a Christian-theist he knows nothing whatsoever as he ought to know about anything. The difference is not that all men alike know certain things about the finite universe and that some claim some additional knowledge while the others do not. On the contrary the Christian-theist must claim that he alone has true knowledge about cows and chickens as well as about God. He does this in no spirit of conceit because it is to himself a gift of God's grace. Nor does he deny that there is knowledge after a fashion that enables the non-theist to get along after a fashion in the world. This is the gift of God's common grace and therefore does not change the absoluteness of the distinction made about the knowledge and the ignorance of the theist and the non-theist respectively.[44]

Christian philosophy must point out that anti-theism destroys knowledge and reason and cannot exist on its own presuppositions. "The autonomous man cannot forever flee back and forth between the arid mountains of timeless logic and the shoreless ocean of pure potentiality. He must at last be brought to bay."[45] In Van Til we have a truly Christian philosophy, one based fully on the presuppositions of Christianity and doing justice to the unity and variety of human ex-

49

perience. Because of its Christian character, it avoids the pitfalls of rationalism and irrationalism. On the basis of the ontological trinity, a truly Christian system is developed of great and far-reaching importance. The issues raised by Van Til are to be reckoned with, and no man can claim to espouse a Christian philosophy without coming to terms with these presuppositions as outlined by Van Til.

We began this survey of Van Til's challenge to epistemology with a story of a naked emperor. We saw that man, naked in his ethical alienation from God, seeks to clothe himself in a metaphysical independence from God. In other words, man seeks to clothe himself by robbing God and leaving Him naked. But the attempt is presumption and an impossibility and only emphasizes the nakedness of man, his ethical rebellion against God and at the same time his total metaphysical dependence upon Him. Man cannot rob God, cannot gain a metaphysical independence, and every claim to autonomy is so much "emperor's clothes," a hollow pretension which only reveals more nakedly the natural man's misshapen nature. Van Til is right, therefore, when he says in effect, as he surveys the natural man and his philosophies, that the emperor has no clothes. He that hath ears to hear, let him hear. In Van Til and in Dooyeweerd, we have the clearest and most consistent formulation of the principles of Christian philosophy. Moreover, because Van Til brings to such clear focus the issues between Christian-theism and anti-theism, his philosophy constitutes a stone of stumbling and a rock of offense (Isa. 8:14) to those whose philosophic concern is to break down the offense of Christianity to the natural man. God and His philosophers call attention to man's nakedness and offer him the robes of God in Christ; the compromisers insist that the natural man is fully clothed; it is only his overcoat that is lacking. This is blindness, not only concerning the natural man, but with regard to themselves and to God. Not only of the emperor but of his philosophers it must be said, "They have no clothes."

CHAPTER 1.
1. Andre Parrot: *The Tower of Babel*, pp. 64, 68. New York: The Philosophical Library, 1955.
2. Eric Burrows, "Some Cosmological Patterns in Babylonian Religion," in S. H. Hooke, ed., *The Labryinth*, Further Studies in the Relation between Myth and Ritual in the Ancient World, p. 53. London: SPCK, 1935.
3. Albert William Levi: *Philosophy and the Modern World*, p. 64. Bloomington: Indiana University Press, 1959.
4. Cited in Levi, p. 557.
CHAPTER 2.
1. All three are published by Eerdmans.
2. All these are published by Presbyterian & Reformed Publishing Co.
CHAPTER 3.
1. Alan Richardson: *Christian Apologetics*, p. 150 (Harper, New York).
2. Intro. to B. B. Warfield, *The Inspiration and Authority of the Bible*, p. 18 (Presbyterian and Reformed, Philadelphia).
3. *Ibid.*, p. 22f.
4. *Ibid.*, p. 35.
5. Van Til: *Christianity in Modern Theology*, pp. 18ff.
6. *Ibid.*, p. 80f.
7. P. 65f., cited in Van Til: *The New Modernism*, p. 173.
8. Van Til: *Christianity and Idealism*, pp. 57-74.
9. *Ibid.*, p. 134.
10. Van Til: *Metaphysics of Apologetics*, p. 12.
11. *Ibid.*, p. 14.
12. *Ibid.*, p. 15.
13. *Ibid.*, p. 16.
14. Van Til: *Metaphysics of Apologetics*, p. 20. Cf. Van Til: "Nature and Scripture" in *The Infallible Word*, pp. 255ff.
15. Van Til: *Metaphysics of Apologetics*, p. 22.
16. *Ibid.*, p. 38.
17. *Ibid.*, p. 46.
18. *Ibid.*, p. 57.
19. Sheen, p. 226 cited in Van Til, *op. cit.*, p. 58.
20. *Ibid.*, p. 66.
21. *Ibid.*, p. 66f.
22. Krauth, The Conservative Reformation and its Theology, p. 350 cited in Van Til, *op. cit.*, p. 65.
23. *Ibid.*, p. 72.
24. *Ibid.*, p. 88.
25. *Ibid.*, p. 99.
26. *Ibid.*, p. 90. When Van Til says that "the principles of unity and diversity must be equally original," this is a *biblical must*, made necessary because God is one God and yet triune. The equal ultimacy of the one and many is directly derived from the doctrine of the Trinity.
27. *Ibid.*, p. 95.
28. *Ibid.*, p. 99.
29. Van Til: "Nature and Scripture" in *The Infallible Word*, p. 285.
30. Van Til: *Metaphysics of Apologetics*, p. 101.
31. Van Til: "Nature and Scripture" from *The Infallible Word*, p. 289.
32. Van Til: *Metaphysics of Apologetics*, p. 103.
33. *Ibid.*, p. 107.
34. *Ibid.*, p. 108.
35. *Ibid.*, p. 110.
36. *Ibid.*, p. 114.
37. *Ibid.*, p. 122.
38. For Van Til's analyses of contemporary philosophies and theologies see *Metaphysics of Apologetics, Defense of the Faith, Christianity and Idealism, Christianity in Modern Theology, The New Modernism*, etc.
39. Van Til: *Metaphysics of Apologetics*, p. 160.
40. Cited by Van Til in *Christian Philosophy*, a pamphlet, quoting E. J. Carnell, *An Introduction to Christian Apologetics* (Eerdmans, Grand Rapids, Mich.).
41. Van Til: *Christian Philosophy*.
42. Van Til: *Metaphysics of Apologetics*, p. 174.
43. *Ibid.*, p. 181b.
44. *Ibid.*, p. 194.
45. Van Til: "Nature and Scripture," p. 293.